Guided Reading Notes

Gold Band
Oxford Level 9

Head to Head

Contents

Introduction	2
Top of the Table (Fiction)	6
Power Racers (Fiction)	13
I'm the Leader! (Fiction)	20
Game On! (Non-fiction)	27
An A–Z of Record Breakers (Non-fiction)	34

Introduction

Why is guided reading important?

Guided reading plays an important role in your whole-school provision for reading, providing opportunities for children to progress and develop the key competencies they need to become confident and skilled independent readers. Working with small groups of children, with texts closely matched to the readers' needs, guided reading is the perfect vehicle for delivering focused teaching from Reception/PI right through to Year 6/P7. The teacher-pupil interaction also provides a valuable assessment opportunity, helping you identify exactly what each child can and can't do. Through guided reading children also encounter a world of exciting, whole books – building a community of readers who read for pleasure.

About *Project X Origins*

Project X Origins is a comprehensive, whole-school guided reading programme designed to help you teach the wide range of skills essential to ensure children progress as readers and to help nurture a love of reading.

Ensuring the key skills are covered

Project X Origins incorporates all of the key skills children need to develop to become successful and enthusiastic readers:

> **Word reading:** phonically regular and common exception words are introduced systematically in the early levels with phonic opportunities provided throughout the notes. As children progress, they are encouraged to use their decoding skills whenever they encounter new or unfamiliar words, and also to recognize how this impacts on different spelling rules.

- **Comprehension:** understanding what has been read is central to being an effective and engaged reader but comprehension is not something that comes automatically so specific strategies have been built into the notes to ensure children develop comprehension skills they can use over a range of texts:
  - Previewing
  - Predicting
  - Activating and building prior knowledge
  - Questioning
  - Recalling
  - Visualizing and other sensory responses
  - Deducting, inferring and drawing conclusions
  - Determining importance
  - Synthesizing
  - Empathizing
  - Summarizing
  - Personal response, including adopting a critical response

- **Reading fluency:** fluency occurs as children develop automatic word recognition, reading with pace and expression. Strategies to help achieve this, including meaningful opportunities for oral reading, re-reading and re-listening are provided throughout.

- **Vocabulary:** introducing new vocabulary within a meaningful context is an important element in extending children's vocabulary range, developing their reading fluency and comprehension. Each thematic cluster provides opportunities for revisiting and reinforcing vocabulary over a range of books and contexts.

- **Grammar, punctuation and spelling:** learning about language in the context of a text, rather than through a series of discrete exercises, can help make grammar, punctuation and spelling relevant and helps children make the link between grammar, punctuation and clarity of meaning, thus supporting their development as writers. Opportunities to support an in-depth look at language are provided for every book from Year 1/P2 to Year 6/P7.

- **Spoken language:** talk is crucial to learning and developing their comprehension so children are given plenty of opportunities to: discuss and debate their ideas with others; justify their opinions; ask and answer questions; explore and hypothesise; summarise, describe and explain; and listen and respond to the ideas of others.

Assessment and progression in reading

Project X Origins includes a rigorous assessment spine drawn from the *Oxford Ros Wilson Reading Criterion Scale* to ensure that you know exactly what each child can do and what they need to focus on next in order to make progress. This assessment framework, combined with the careful levelling of the Oxford Levels, will help you select the right book with the right level of challenge for each of your guided reading groups and to assess, track and monitor each child's progress.

Step 1

On a termly basis, use the *Reading Criterion Scale* (which can be found in the relevant *Project X Origins Teaching Handbook*) to assess each child's reading. The scale will tell you the Oxford Level a child is comfortable reading at, and the areas a child needs to develop. You can also use this assessment to form your guided reading groups.

Step 2

Plan your guided reading sessions by selecting books at the appropriate Oxford Level that focus on the relevant learning needs of the group. You will find charts showing the learning objectives and assessment points for every *Project X Origins* book in the relevant *Project X Origins Teaching Handbook*. Depending on your assessment, you might choose a book at the level the children are comfortable at or one from the next level up, to offer some stretch.

Step 3

Use the assessment points within the Guided Reading Notes to support on-going assessment of children's reading progress. The Progress Tracking Charts in the relevant *Project X Origins Teaching Handbook* can be used to record this if you wish. Regularly re-assess each child's progress combining your on-going informal assessments and the termly assessment using the *Reading Criterion Scale*. Use this information to re-organize guided reading groups and teaching plans in response to children's varying degrees of progress.

Getting started: using the Guided Reading Notes

At a glance
Project X Origins Guided Reading Notes offer detailed guidance to help deliver effective and engaging guided reading sessions, and are designed to be used flexibly to ensure you get the most out of each book. For notes containing multiple sessions, you may choose to focus on each of these sessions or focus on one session and have the children read the rest of the book independently.

Curricula correlation and assessment
At the beginning of every set of notes there are correlation charts for all UK curricula, ensuring that across the clusters the main curricula objectives are covered. In addition, an overview of assessment points for each book is provided – these points are also signposted throughout the notes.

Key information
Before the first session, an overview of the book and the resources you will need (such as additional photocopy masters) is provided.

Teaching sequence
Each guided reading session follows the same teaching sequence:
- **Before reading**: children explore the context of each book to support their understanding and help them engage with the text. They are encouraged to discuss, recall, respond, predict and speculate about the book. Opportunities to focus on word reading and/or vocabulary are also introduced at this point.
- **During reading**: children are given a section of the book to read with specific questions in mind.
- **After reading**: children reflect on and discuss what they have read. They are encouraged to delve deeper, exploring their understanding of the text, developing their vocabulary, grammar, punctuation, spelling and fluency where appropriate.
- **Follow-up**: opportunities for children to extend their learning outside the session are provided, including writing and cross-curricular activities.

Throughout the sessions, the key strategies that children are developing are clearly identified.

Top of the Table
BY CHRIS POWLING

Curricula correlation

English National Curriculum

Spoken language	Maintain attention and participate actively in collaborative conversations, staying on topic and initiating and responding to comments
Word reading	Read aloud books closely matched to their improving phonic knowledge, sounding out unfamiliar words accurately, automatically and without undue hesitation
	Read accurately words of two or more syllables
Comprehension	Discuss the sequence of events in books and how items of information are related
	Make inferences on the basis of what is being said and done

Phonics and vocabulary

GPCs	/ee/ beat, real, easily, season, cheer, Greenville, believe, here
Decodable 2 and 3 syllable words	football, winner, plastic, upset, outside, afternoon, bedroom, expert, Greenville, Woodside
Common exception words	can't, play, looking, top, more, after, shouted, school
Challenge and context words	match, league, breaks, idea, answered, whistle, decide, eyes, suspiciously, minute, special

Grammar, punctuation and spelling

Grammar and Punctuation	Co-ordination	He kicked it hard but he didn't score. He rotated the poles and moved the players like an expert.
Spelling	Contractions	we'll, won't, don't, I'd

Reading assessment points

Word reading	Can the children use syllables to read unknown polysyllabic words, including knowledge of common prefixes and suffixes?
	Can the children read words with contractions, e.g. I'm, I'll, we'll, and understand that the apostrophe represents the omitted letter(s)?
Comprehension	Can the children make predictions about a text using a range of clues?
	Are the children beginning to read between the lines, using clues from text and pictures, to discuss thoughts, feelings and actions?
	Can the children provide simple explanations about events or information?
	Can the children summarise a story, giving the main points clearly in sequence?

Scottish Curriculum for Excellence

Listening and talking	When I engage with others, I know when and how to listen, when to talk, how much to say, when to ask questions and how to respond with respect LIT 1-02a
Reading	I can use my knowledge of sight vocabulary, phonics, context clues, punctuation and grammar to read with understanding and expression ENG 1-12a
	To show my understanding, I can respond to different kinds of questions and other close reading tasks and I am learning to create some questions of my own ENG 1-17a

Welsh National Literacy Framework

Oracy	Contribute to discussion, keeping a focus on the topic and taking turns to speak (Collaboration and discussion)
Reading	Apply the following reading strategies with increasing frequency to a range of familiar and unfamiliar texts: phonic strategies; recognition of high-frequency words; context clues, e.g. prior knowledge; graphic and syntactic clues; self-correction, including re-reading and reading ahead (Reading strategies)
	Express views about information and details in a text (Response and analysis)
	Recall and retell narratives and information from texts with some details (Comprehension)

Northern Ireland Curriculum

Talking and Listening	Listen to, respond to and explore stories, poems, songs, drama, and media texts through the use of traditional and digital resources and recreate parts of them in a range of expressive activities
Reading	Use a range of strategies to identify unfamiliar words
	Use a range of comprehension skills, both oral and written, to interpret and discuss texts

Top of the Table

About this book

The league final football match may be cancelled due to bad weather. Ant suggests the children play table football. Cat and Tiger shrink and have a penalty shoot-out before the weather clears up and the real game takes place.

You will need

- *Football glossary* Photocopy Master, *Teaching Handbook* for Year 2/P3
- *Penalty shoot-out* Photocopy Master, *Teaching Handbook* for Year 2/P3

▷ Before reading

- Look at the cover and ask the children what they think the story will be about. **(predicting)**

Assessment point
Can the children make predictions about a text using a range of clues?

- Do any of the children play football? Do the girls play football? Have the children seen or played table football? Look at the pictures and ensure that everyone knows the principles. Talk about the skills needed to play successfully. How different is it from real football? **(activating prior knowledge)**

- Look at pages 2–3 together. Do the children understand what is meant by a league table? Can they make the link with the title? **(previewing the text, building prior knowledge)**

- How might the weather affect the match? Have the children ever had an event they were looking forward to being affected by the weather? **(personal response)**

- The story has a number of football terms. Check that the children understand the meaning of the terms and ask them to note any they are unsure of as they read. **(developing vocabulary)**

- Read from page 4 to the end of Chapter 2. What can the children infer about the changing moods of the characters? What aspects of the text and illustrations did they use to come to this understanding? **(empathizing, deducing, inferring, drawing conclusions)**

Assessment point
Are the children beginning to read between the lines, using clues from text and pictures, to discuss thoughts, feelings and actions?

- Ask the children what to do if they encounter a difficult word, modelling with an example from the book.
- Discuss with the children what to do if they struggle to understand the meaning of a word or a sentence, e.g. rereading the word or sentence again.

Assessment point
Can the children use syllables to read unknown polysyllabic words, including knowledge of common prefixes and suffixes?

Phonic opportunity

- Draw attention to all of the words with the /**ee**/ phoneme: *beat, real, easily, season, cheer, Greenville, believe, here.* Ask children to identify the phoneme /ee/ in the words. Support children to say each phoneme and then blend the phonemes to read the word. Ask children to think of other words with the /ee/ sound.
- You may also wish to point out some of the common exception words or practise decoding some of the challenge and context words in this book.

During reading

- Ask the children to read from Chapter 3 to the end of the book.
- As they read, ask them to look for clues in the text to help them understand how the characters are feeling and thinking.
- Also ask the children to look out for the words *and* and *but*. Make a note of where they appear.

After reading

Returning to the text

- What is Ant's idea for Cat and Tiger to see who is the best player? **(recall)**
- Why do Cat and Tiger both miss their final shot in the penalty shoot-out? **(recall, deducing, inferring, drawing conclusions)**
- Why does the football match eventually go ahead? **(recall)**
- What was the final score? Who scored the winning goal? **(recall, deducing, inferring, drawing conclusions)**

Assessment point
Can the children provide simple explanations about events or information?

Developing comprehension

- Ask the children to recall the events of the day from the point of view of Max or Ant. **(summarizing)**
- Can they suggest why Max's heart sank (p.15)? Use hot seating to ask Max what he was thinking at this moment. **(empathizing)**
- Look at the text and illustrations on pages 16–19. Ask the children to work in pairs to make a series of freeze frames to show the facial expressions and body language that Cat and Tiger might use when they miss their final goals in the penalty shoot-out. Using the *Penalty shoot-out* Photocopy Master, ask the children to complete thought bubbles to show what they are thinking at these moments. **(deducing, inferring, drawing conclusions, empathizing)**

Assessment point
Can the children summarise a story, giving the main points clearly in sequence?

Developing vocabulary

- Are there any football terms that the children didn't understand as they read through. Discuss the meaning of these.
- Ask the children, in pairs, to come up with some definitions for the terms on the *Football glossary* Photocopy Master to form an accompanying glossary for other children.

Developing grammar, punctuation and spelling

- Look at page 6 and ask the children to identify the sentence that uses the word *and*. Discuss that this is an example of co-ordination. The word *and* joins groups of words (clauses) that are of the same importance in the sentence. Do the same with the sentence on page 11 using the word *but*. Challenge children to identify another example of this in the book.

- Turn to page 3. Point out the word *we'll*. Explain how this is a contraction and the appostrophe represents missing letters. If it was written in full, it would say *we will*. Can the children guess what *won't* would be if it was written in full?

Assessment point
Can the children read words with contractions, e.g. I'm, I'll, we'll, and understand that the apostrophe represents the omitted letter(s)?

Chapter 3 – The shoot-out

Ant's idea was to have a penalty shoot-out. Cat and Tiger would take it in turns to have five shots each. Ant would work the plastic goalie.
   "The winner will be the one who scores most goals," Max explained. "I'll be referee."

"I'm bound to be the winner!" Tiger boasted.
   Tiger placed the ball on the penalty spot.
   Max blew a whistle. Tiger ran towards the ball. He kicked it hard, but he didn't score. The plastic goalie stopped the ball – with a tap from Ant.

❯ Follow-up

Writing activities

- Ask the children to look outside and then write a short weather forecast based on what they see. **(short writing task)**
- Write a report for the Greenville School newsletter about this football match. Alternatively, if possible, watch a football match at your own school and write a report about it. **(longer writing task)**
- In pairs, discuss the instructions for playing table football and then write a leaflet to explain them. **(spoken language)**

Other literacy activities

- Create a football chant and explore some expressive ways of presenting it chorally. **(spoken language)**

Cross-curricular activities

- Use an Internet search engine to find a weather forecast for your area. **(Computing)**
- Look at the number patterns created by the 11 players on a football table. Investigate the different ways they could be arranged. **(Maths)**
- Hold your own penalty shoot-out. **(PE)**
- In circle time, talk about sensitivity towards other people's feelings and how being able to empathize might affect how we behave. **(PSHE)**

Power Racers
BY SHOO RAYNER

Curricula correlation

English National Curriculum

Spoken language	Use relevant strategies to build their vocabulary
Word reading	Continue to apply phonic knowledge and skills as the route to decode words
Comprehension	Predict what might happen on the basis of what is being said and done
	Recognize simple recurring literary language in stories
	Explain and discuss their understanding of books

Phonics and vocabulary

GPCs	/ai/ race, gave, weight, play, drainpipe, great
Decodable 2 and 3 syllable words	workbench, concrete, overtake, seesaw, helmet, trigger, tunnels, drainpipe, together, apart
Common exception words	box, I'll, fast, girls, car, play, small, take, something
Challenge and context words	racing, garage, knocked, pieces, switched, engines, concrete, bounced, silence, weight

Grammar, punctuation and spelling

Grammar and Punctuation	Use of capital letters, full stops, question marks and exclamation marks to demarcate sentences	Wow! Electric racing cars! "Can we play with them?" said Tiger Don't drive too fast!
Spelling	Adding -ed to words of one syllable ending vowel consonant	strapped, revved, nodded, flipped, jabbed, stopped, dropped, skidded, fitted

Reading assessment points

Word reading	Can the children use a range of phonics strategies to read unknown regular words?
	Do the children know the function of full stops when reading and can they show this in their reading aloud?
Comprehension	Can the children make predictions about a text using a range of clues?
	Can the children provide simple explanations about events or information?
	Can the children discuss reasons for events in stories by beginning to use clues in the story?
	Can the children explain the meaning of 'WOW' words in context (appropriate level of book)?

Scottish Curriculum for Excellence

Listening and talking	I am exploring how pace, gesture, expression, emphasis and choice of words are used to engage others, and I can use what I learn ENG 1-03a
Reading	I can use my knowledge of sight vocabulary, phonics, context clues, punctuation and grammar to read with understanding and expression ENG 1-12a
	I regularly select and read, listen to or watch texts which I enjoy and find interesting, and I can explain why I prefer certain texts and authors LIT 1-11a

Welsh National Literacy Framework

Oracy	Express opinions, giving reasons, and provide appropriate answers to questions (Speaking)
Reading	Apply the following reading strategies with increasing frequency to a range of familiar and unfamiliar texts: phonic strategies; recognition of high-frequency words; context clues, e.g. prior knowledge; graphic and syntactic clues; self-correction, including re-reading and reading ahead (Reading strategies)
	Express views about information and details in a text (Response and analysis)
	Read aloud with attention to punctuation, including full stops, question, exclamation and speech marks, varying intonation, voice and pace (Reading strategies)

Northern Ireland Curriculum

Talking and Listening	Take turns at talking and listening in group and paired activities
Reading	Use a range of strategies to identify unfamiliar words
	Express opinions and give reasons based on what they have read

About this book

When Tiger's dad finds an old electric-car racing game in the garage, it leads to a head to head race between Cat and Tiger – as micro-sized drivers! Who will win?

You will need

- *Speed dominoes* Photocopy Master, *Teaching Handbook* for Year 2/P3
- *Story talk frame* Photocopy Master, *Teaching Handbook* for Year 2/P3

▶ Before reading

- Ask the children if they have ever seen or played with an electric car racing set. What was it like? **(activating prior knowledge)**
- Look at the cover of the book and talk about the title. What might this story be about? **(predicting)**
- Ask the children to look at the pictures and comment on the aspects of safety when racing cars – crash helmets, seat belts, etc. Why are they important for racing drivers? Are there any other things that help to make racing safer? **(previewing the text)**
- Read Chapter 1 together. Ask the children what they would do next, if they were one of the children. Will it make a difference if Tiger's dad won't be present in the garage in the next chapter? Why? **(synthesizing)**
- Read Chapter 2 together. Can the children imagine what it would be like to be small enough to fit into one of the racing cars? **(visualizing and other sensory responses)**
- Ask the children what to do if they encounter a difficult word, modelling with an example from the book.
- Discuss with the children what to do if they struggle to understand the meaning of a word or a sentence, e.g. rereading the word or sentence again.

Assessment point

Can the children make predictions about a text using a range of clues?

Phonic opportunity

- Draw attention to all of the words with the /**ai**/ phoneme: *race, gave, weight, play, drainpipe, great*. Ask the children to identify the phoneme /ai/ in the words. Support children to say each phoneme and then blend the phonemes to read the word. Ask the children to think of other words with the /ai/ sound.
- You may also wish to point out some of the common exception words or practise decoding some of the challenge and context words in this book.

Assessment point
Can the children use a range of phonics strategies to read unknown regular words?

During reading

- Ask the children to read from Chapter 3 to the end of the book.
- As they read, ask them to think about words that the author has chosen to give the feeling of speed and danger.
- Also, ask the children to look out for how sentences begin and end, e.g. capital letters, full stops and question marks.

After reading

Returning to the text

- Ask the children which bit of the race they thought was the most exciting. When was it the most dangerous? Why? **(recall, personal response, determining importance)**
- What are the main safety concerns Cat and Ant have about being micro-drivers? How do they solve the problems? **(recall)**
- Why would the drainpipe be like a tunnel? **(visualizing)**
- Can the children demonstrate what happened when the cars landed on the plank of wood that acted like a seesaw? **(visualizing and other sensory responses)**
- Why do they think Tiger winks at Cat at the end of the story? **(deducing, (inferring, drawing conclusions)**

Assessment point
Can the children provide simple explanations about events or information?

Developing comprehension

- Ask the children why they think the author chose to have Tiger's dad take the rubbish to the dump.
- Thinking in role as the characters, can the children think of ways to explain to Tiger's dad why the garage is in a mess? If they tell him the truth, will he believe them? Role play the scene with you in role as Tiger's dad. How will the children tailor their version of the events? **(questioning, personal response)**

Assessment point
Can the children discuss reasons for events in stories by beginning to use clues in the story?

Developing vocabulary

- Ask the children if they can recall any interesting words from the story that were used to give a feeling of speed or danger. How effective do they think they are? Add these to the word wall. Ask the children, in pairs, to select a word and use a thesaurus (either a book or on a computer) to find alternatives. Can they substitute their new word in the text? Which word is the better word – the original or the substitute?
- Ask the children if they can think of some verbs that might be used to talk about racing cars. Collect their ideas on a word wall. Turn them into the past tense. Identify any verbs that need to have the last letter doubled before adding the suffix. The children could use the *Speed dominoes* Photocopy Master to reinforce this.

Assessment point
Can the children explain the meaning of 'WOW' words in context (appropriate level of book)?

Developing grammar, punctuation and spelling

- Write some of the sentences from the book on the board and remind the children of the importance of using capital letters and full stops in sentences. When might they replace a full stop with a question mark or an exclamation mark?

- Draw the children's attention to the word *fitted* on page 5. Ask the children to identify the root word *(fit)*. Look at other examples where there is a double consonant before the *-ed*. Discuss the spelling rule: if a one-syllable verb has a short vowel sound and ends in a consonant you need to double the consonant before adding *-ed*. Explain that this rule can also be applied to adding *-ing*, *-er*, *-est* and *-y* to words that end in an 'e'.

Assessment point

Do the children know the function of full stops when reading and can they show this in their reading aloud?

Developing fluency

- Ask the children to look again at Chapter 3 and try reading aloud some of the speech, modelling the way that it would sound with and without an exclamation mark.

❯ Follow-up

Writing activities

- Create a poster explaining why people should wear a seat belt when they go in a car. **(short writing task)**
- In pairs, ask the children to make a story map, or use the *Story talk frame* Photocopy Master, then orally retell the story as if they were either Cat or Tiger before writing their own version. **(longer writing task)**
- Write a short letter to Tiger's dad saying sorry about the mess in the garage. **(short writing task)**

Other literacy activities

- Tiger says *"Girls can't drive!"* Have a discussion about whether there are some things that girls or boys can or can't do. **(spoken language)**
- Use various information texts to find out about famous racing drivers.

Cross-curricular activities

- Build an obstacle course for playing with model cars. Include features such as a seesaw and a drainpipe. **(DT)**
- Make a ramp for a toy car to run down. Investigate how different surfaces affect the car's speed. **(Science)**
- Find out about the first cars in Britain. How fast could they go? **(History)**

I'm the Leader!
BY TONY BRADMAN

Curricula correlation

English National Curriculum

Spoken language	Use spoken language to develop understanding through speculating, hypothesising, imagining and exploring ideas
Word reading	Read most words quickly and accurately when they have been frequently encountered without overt sounding and blending
Comprehension	Make inferences on the basis of what is said and done
	Predict what might happen on the basis of what has been read so far
	Discuss the sequence of events in books and how items of information are related

Phonics and vocabulary

GPCs	/igh/ kind, micro-den, nearby, like, decided, hide, magpie, high, right
Decodable 2 and 3 syllable words	somebody, something, leader, shadow, carefully, nearby
Common exception words	eat, thought, there, called, shouted, fast, eyes
Challenge and context words	trouble, whispered, invention, idea, tangled, ache, eyes, knew, watered

Grammar, punctuation and spelling

Grammar and Punctuation	Suffix -ed	started, opened, snapped, tried, wanted
Spelling	Adding -ed to verbs where no change needed to root word	started, opened, snapped, wanted, stomped, gasped, tried
	Adding -ed to verbs ending in consonant -y	

Reading assessment points

Word reading	Can the children use a range of phonics strategies to read unknown regular words?
Comprehension	Can the children make predictions about a text using a range of clues?
	Can the children provide simple explanations about events or information?
	Can the children comment on obvious characteristics and actions of characters in stories?
	Are the children beginning to read between the lines, using clues from text and pictures, to discuss thoughts, feelings and actions?
	Can the children summarise a story, giving the main points clearly in sequence?
	Can the children discuss reasons for events in stories by beginning to use clues in the story?

Scottish Curriculum for Excellence

Listening and talking	When listening and talking with others for different purposes, I can exchange information, experiences, explanations, ideas and opinions, and clarify points by asking questions or by asking others to say more LIT 1-09a
Reading	I can use my knowledge of sight vocabulary, phonics, context clues, punctuation and grammar to read with understanding and expression ENG 1-12a
	I can share my thoughts about structure, characters and/or setting, recognise the writer's message and relate it to my own experiences, and comment on the effective choice of words and other features ENG 1-19a

Welsh National Literacy Framework

Oracy	Share activities and information to complete a task (Collaboration and discussion)
Reading	Apply the following reading strategies with increasing frequency to a range of familiar and unfamiliar texts: phonic strategies; recognition of high-frequency words; context clues, e.g. prior knowledge; graphic and syntactic clues; self-correction, including re-reading and reading ahead (Reading strategies)
	Express views about information and details in a text (Response and analysis)

Northern Ireland Curriculum

Talking and Listening	Listen to, respond to and explore stories, poems, songs, drama, and media texts through the use of traditional and digital resources and recreate parts of them in a range of expressive activities
Reading	Use a range of strategies to identify unfamiliar words
	Express opinions and give reasons based on what they have read

I'm the Leader!

About this book

Max and Tiger fall out over who should be the leader. Although Cat and Ant try to pacify them, Max stomps off leaving Tiger to be the leader. Trouble soon befalls the remaining three when a magpie siezes Cat. Tiger realizes that leadership isn't easy. Max saves the day when he returns on his new invention – a hover board.

You will need

- *Lead on!* Photocopy Master, *Teaching Handbook* for Year 2/P3

▶ Before reading

- Look at the cover together. What is going on? What might Tiger and the magpie be thinking? What could have happened a few minutes earlier? What might happen next? **(predicting)**

Assessment point

Can the children make predictions about a text using a range of clues?

- Look at page 3 and read the text. Have the children ever seen a magpie? What can they tell you about magpies? Can they name any other creatures that are omnivorous? **(previewing the text, activating prior knowledge)**
- Read page 4 together. What job do the children think Max might have for Tiger? **(predicting)**
- Read on to page 7. Ask the children if they have ever been involved in an argument with a friend. How did it feel? **(empathizing)**
- Read to the end of page 11 together. What do the children think will happen next? Do they know what a cliffhanger is? Start a story map together. **(determining importance)**
- Talk about the way chapters work. Do they think page 11 could be the end of a chapter? Turn over to see and discuss where the end of the chapter comes on page 13. Is this a good place to end the chapter? Add developments to the story map. **(determining importance)**
- Ask the children what to do if they encounter a difficult word, modelling with an example from the book.
- Discuss with the children what to do if they struggle to understand the meaning of a word or a sentence, e.g. rereading the word or sentence again.

> *Phonic opportunity*
> - Draw attention to all of the words with the /**igh**/ phoneme: *kind, micro-den, nearby, like, decided, hide, magpie, high, right*. Ask children to identify the phoneme /igh/ in the words. Support children to say each phoneme and then blend the phonemes to read the word. Ask children to think of other words with the /igh/ sound.
> - You may also wish to point out some of the common exception words or practise decoding some of the challenge and context words in this book.

During reading

- Can the children use a range of phonics strategies to read unknown regular words?
- As they read, ask them to notice where Chapters 3 and 4 end and how they, as readers, feel at those points.
- Also ask the children to look out for words with the *-ed* suffix as they read.

Assessment point
Can the children use a range of phonics strategies to read unknown regular words?

After reading

Returning to the text

- Ask the children why the magpie seized Cat. **(recall)**
- What is so scary about the magpie? **(personal response)**
- Can the children picture what it would be like to be Cat in the magpie's nest? How would they have felt when they saw the magpie returning? **(visualizing and other sensory responses, empathizing)**
- Tiger wants to test the hover board. Can they suggest other things Tiger could say in his response to Max? **(deducing, inferring, drawing conclusions)**

Assessment point
Can the children provide simple explanations about events or information?

Assessment point
Can the children comment on obvious characteristics and actions of characters in stories?

Developing comprehension

- Return to the end of Chapter 3. How did the children, as readers, feel at this point? **(empathizing)**
- Similarly, refer to the end of Chapters 4 and 5. In what ways were their feelings different at the end of each chapter? Ask the children, in pairs, to complete their own story maps. **(personal response)**
- Later, the children could use their story maps to retell the story to each other. **(summarizing)**
- What do the children think about the way Tiger acted as a leader in this situation? Could he have saved Cat on his own? What advice would they have given Tiger? **(empathizing, personal response, adopting a critical stance)**
- Ask the children to role play alternative solutions Tiger could have made to solve the problem.
- Invite the children to rewrite the section of the story where Tiger tries to act as leader, using one of the group's ideas. Remind them that what Tiger says and does will change the following course of action.

Assessment point

Are the children beginning to read between the lines, using clues from text and pictures, to discuss thoughts, feelings and actions?

Assessment point

Can the children summarise a story, giving the main points clearly in sequence?

Assessment point

Can the children discuss reasons for events in stories by beginning to use clues in the story?

Developing grammar, punctuation and spelling

- Look at the verbs the children collected ending in *-ed*. Explain that the suffix *-ed* shows that the action happened in the past tense. Using the word *started*, can they children identify the root verb (*start*). Talk about how there is no change to the verb in some cases, e.g. *started*, *stomped*, *wanted*. Now look at *tried*. Explain that if the root verb ends with a 'y', the 'y' is replaced by an 'i' before the *-ed* is added. Write down some more examples of this together, taking off the 'y', adding 'i' and then *-ed*, e.g. *copy–copied*, *cry–cried*.

Tiger felt his stomach lurch as he rose into the air. He quickly flew back to Ant.

Ant pointed to a nearby tree. "Up there," he called.

Tiger steered carefully between the tangled branches. He saw Cat's yellow jumper through the green leaves.

"Help!" Cat shouted, when she saw him.

The nest was full of shiny things the magpie had taken. But the magpie was nowhere to be seen.

"Are you OK?" Tiger asked.

"Yes," said Cat, shakily. "But I thought that bird was going to eat me!"

"Nah … You would probably give it tummy ache!" smiled Tiger.

Cat scowled at him.

Follow-up

Writing activities
- Make a drawing of the hover board with a caption and labels to identify its features. **(short writing task)**
- Ask the children to write their own version of a well-known traditional tale changing what a character says or does to something different, thereby changing the course of action. **(longer writing task)**
- Write a postcard to Max telling him what they think of his hover board invention. **(short writing task)**

Other literacy activities
- If possible, provide a book box containing a wide range of reading material (fiction and non-fiction) that deals with leadership. Allow time for children to explore and talk about what they have read. They could fill in the 'cards' on the *Lead on!* Photocopy Master.
- Make a vocabulary poster with words and phrases that could be used to describe a good leader. **(vocabulary)**

Cross-curricular activities
- Children could hang a bird feeder where they can observe birds that visit. Encourage them in their observations and provide information texts to support them in finding out more about specific birds. **(Science)**
- Sort a collection of junk materials. Which wold the magpie be interested in? What are they made of? **(Science)**
- Make a hover board from junk materials. Children could also consider making a micro-sized one to use in small world play. **(DT)**
- In circle time, discuss what makes a good leader, how to deal with disagreements and how to share roles and responsibilities. **(PSHE)**

Game On!
BY JANE PENROSE

Curricula correlation
English National Curriculum

Spoken language	Give well-structured descriptions and explanations
Word reading	Re-read books to build up their fluency and confidence in word reading
Comprehension	Discuss their favourite words and phrases
	Explain and discuss their understanidng of books
	Check that the text makes sense to them as they read and correct inaccurate reading

Phonics and vocabulary

GPCs	/ee/ Greece, read, team, these
Decodable 2 and 3 syllable words	enjoy, boxing, modern, football, sensors, helmet, cockpit, sportspeople, different
Common exception words	has, play, every, around, inside, with
Challenge and context words	ancient, Olympics, invention, world, soldiers, dangerous, imagine, hour, wheel, tournament, knight, Paralympic

Grammar, punctuation and spelling

Grammar and Punctuation	Expanded noun phrases for description and specification	new invention, Ancient Rome, largest sporting event, very hot day, world's most popular sport, virtual reality helmet, very competitive event
Spelling	Words ending in -tion	invention, competition, instruction, situation

Reading assessment points

Word reading	Can the children identify when reading does not make sense and self-corrects in order for the text to make sense?
Comprehension	Can the children make predictions about a text using a range of clues?
	Are the children beginning to use contents and index pages to locate information in non-fiction texts?
	Can the children provide simple explanations about events or information?
	Are the children beginning to talk about the features of certain non-fiction texts?
	Can the children talk about how different words and phrases affect meaning?

Scottish Curriculum for Excellence

Listening and talking	I can select ideas and relevant information, organise these in a logical sequence and use words which will be interesting and/or useful for others LIT 1-06a
Reading	I can use my knowledge of sight vocabulary, phonics, context clues, punctuation and grammar to read with understanding and expression ENG 1-12a
	I can share my thoughts about structure, characters and/or setting, recognise the writer's message and relate it to my own experiences, and comment on the effective choice of words and other features ENG 1-19a

Welsh National Literacy Framework

Oracy	Extend their ideas or accounts by sequencing what they say and including relevant details (Speaking)
Reading	Explain relevant details from texts (Comprehension)
	Show understanding and express opinions about language, information and events in texts (Response and analysis)
	Use the different features of texts to make meaning, e.g. pictures, charts and layout (Reading strategies)

Northern Ireland Curriculum

Talking and Listening	Present ideas and information with some structure and sequence
Reading	Use a range of strategies to identify unfamiliar words
	Read, explore, understand and make use of a range of traditional and digital texts

About this book

Modern day and historical versions of the Olympic Games, racing, football, board games and computer games are compared and contrasted.

You will need
- *Fun with words* Photocopy Master, *Teaching Handbook* for Year 2/P3
- Chess set, Snakes and ladders game

▸ Before reading

- Look at the cover together. What does the title suggest about the content of the book? **(predicting)**

  > **Assessment point**
  > Can the children make predictions about a text using a range of clues?

- Turn to the contents page and ensure that everyone understands how it can be used to support their reading. Invite suggestions as to the organization of the text, based on their ability to make inferences from the content headings. **(activating and building prior knowledge)**

- Ask the children what they might expect to read about on pages 14 and 15. Turn to those pages – are they right? Draw their attention to the word *Referees* in bold and remind them how the meaning of the word can be found in the glossary on page 24. **(predicting, activating prior knowledge)**

- Can the children explain the different ways the contents, the glossary and the index support the reading of a non-fiction text? **(building prior knowledge)**

  > **Assessment point**
  > Are the children beginning to use contents and index pages to locate information in non-fiction texts?

- Ask the children to identify a word from the glossary that they are unfamiliar with. Ask them to read the definition and share that word and their understanding of it with a partner. **(word reading)**

- Read the section on the ancient Olympics together. Model how the pages can be read in a non-linear way. **(developing fluency)**

- Direct the children to read pages 6–7 in pairs. Can they come up with some similarities and differences between the ancient and modern Olympics? Which event would they like to be able to watch or take part in? Why? **(personal response)**

- Ask the children what to do if they encounter a difficult word, modelling with an example from the book.

- Discuss with the children what to do if they struggle to understand the meaning of a word or a sentence, e.g. rereading the word or sentence again.

> **Assessment point**
> Can the children identify when reading does not make sense and self-corrects in order for the text to make sense?

Phonic opportunity

- On pages 4–5 and 8–9 there are some common exception words. Can the children use their phonic knowledge to work out how to say them?
- You may also wish to point out some of the other common exception words elsewhere in the book or practise decoding some of the challenge and context words.

During reading

- Ask the children to read from page 8 to the end of the book, using the contents page to select the games they are most interested in reading first.
- As they read, ask them to use the glossary to check any unfamiliar words.
- Also ask the children to look out for words ending in *-tion*.

> **Assessment point**
> Are the children beginning to use contents and index pages to locate information in non-fiction texts?

After reading

Returning to the text

- Ask the children which game or sport they found most interesting and to say why. **(recall, personal response)**
- There are several references to going 'head to head'. What is their understanding of this expression? **(deducing, inferring, drawing conclusions, synthesizing)**
- Show the children a chessboard. Invite them to show each other how the different pieces move on it, based on their understanding of the chart on page 17. **(synthesizing)**

- Can the children imagine what a virtual helmet would be like? How could one be used to help train fire officers? Ask them to shut their eyes. Describe a scene to them, perhaps from the chariot racing or mob football sections. Taking it in turns, allow each child in the group to choose a place in the book and describe a scene, while the other children close their eyes and imagine the scene using all their senses. **(visualizing and other sensory responses)**

Developing comprehension

- Ask the children to recall the ways that football has changed over time. What might have been the reasons for the changes? How did the pictures and text features help their understanding? **(visualizing, deducing, inferring, drawing conclusions)**

Assessment point
Can the children provide simple explanations about events or information?

- Look at page 18. Have the children played Snakes and ladders? Explain to the children that they will, either in pairs or small groups, produce a booklet about a favourite board game or computer game.

- Ask them to choose the game and discuss how the booklet will be presented. Remind them to think about the reader and select from a variety of appropriate organizational features that are appropriate for presenting their chosen subject matter.

Assessment point
Are the children beginning to talk about the features of certain non-fiction texts?

Developing vocabulary

- Refer the children to the heading *'Bored? Get out the board!'* on page 16. Do they recognize the writer's intended word play? Can they think of any other words that sound the same but have different spellings and meanings? Begin a word bank that could be developed as a follow-up activity.

Developing grammar, punctuation and spelling

- Look at the words the children collected ending in -tion. Explain that this letter string makes the sound /shun/.
- Write the word *water* on the board and ask the children to explain what picture they have in their heads. Now Write *large puddle of dirty, smelly water* on the board and ask them how their image has changed. Discuss how the expanded noun phrase adds detail and makes the information more specific for the reader. Discuss how this helps to visualise the action. Challenge children to look through the book and identify other examples of expanded noun phrases that add specific details, e.g. *new invention*.

Assessment point
Can the children talk about how different words and phrases affect meaning?

❯ Follow-up

Writing activities

- Ask the children to work in pairs and choose one of the games/sports to focus on. Using freeze frames, encourage them to create two 'snapshots' that encapsulate the differences between the 'then and now' aspects. If possible, take a digital photograph of each. Children then write short explanations to go with each one. **(short writing task)**
- Allow the children to write their booklet about a board game or computer game after they have planned it together. **(longer writing task)**
- Write a list of instructions or rules for a playground game. **(short writing task)**

Other literacy activities

- Provide a selection of simple (and appropriate) joke books for children to find jokes that use word play/puns. Make a collection of those they like most, sharing them orally. Children can then try creating their own jokes based on homophones, using the *Fun with words* Photocopy Master. **(spoken language)**

Cross-curricular activities

- Invite the children to design their own board game, make it, write instructions for it, then play it with each other. **(DT)**
- Hold a mini Olympics with children deciding which sports should be included. Winners could be awarded 'laurel wreaths'. **(PE)**
- Collect a range of board games that can be kept in the classroom for children to play in collaborative groups. **(PSHE)**

An A–Z of Record Breakers
BY CHLOE RHODES

Curricula correlation
English National Curriculum

Spoken language	Maintain attention and participate actively in collaborative conversations, staying on topic and initiating and responding to comments
Word reading	Read accurately words of two or more syllables
Comprehension	Read non-fiction books that are structured in different ways
	Draw on what they already know or on background information and vocabulary provided by the teacher

Phonics and vocabulary

GPCs	/igh/ bright, high, kite, dive, bike, miles, by, trying
Decodable 2 and 3 syllable words	leapfrog, hopscotch, igloo, chopsticks, jelly, person, domino, platform, balloon
Common exception words	when, where, who, first, long, inside, across, around
Challenge and context words	earth, cycling, weighed, scientists, engineers, succeed, mountaineering, climbers, ocean, aeroplane, machine, yachting

Grammar, punctuation and spelling

Grammar and Punctuation	Use of the suffix -est in adjectives	coldest, windiest, shortest, longest, heaviest, biggest, greatest, highest, youngest, latest
Spelling	The /dj/ sound spelt as -ge and -dge	oxygen, managed, judge, passenger, change, Germany, aged

Reading assessment points

Word reading	Can the children identify when reading does not make sense and self-corrects in order for the text to make sense?
Comprehension	Can the children make predictions about a text using a range of clues?
	Can the children talk about the features of certain non-fiction texts?
	Can the children provide simple explanations about events or information?
	Can the children locate specific information on a given page in response to a direct question?
	Can the children relate stories/texts to their own experiences, including story settings and incidents?

Scottish Curriculum for Excellence

Listening and talking	When I engage with others, I know when and how to listen, when to talk, how much to say, when to ask questions and how to respond with respect LIT I-02a
Reading	I can use my knowledge of sight vocabulary, phonics, context clues, punctuation and grammar to read with understanding and expression ENG I-I2a
	Using what I know about the features of different types of texts, I can find, select, sort and use information for a specific purpose LIT-I4a

Welsh National Literacy Framework

Oracy	Express opinions, giving reasons, and provide appropriate answers to questions (Speaking)
Reading	Apply the following reading strategies with increasing frequency to a range of familiar and unfamiliar texts: phonic strategies; recognition of high-frequency words; context clues, e.g. prior knowledge; graphic and syntactic clues; self-correction, including re-reading and reading ahead (Reading strategies)
	Identify and use text features, e.g. titles, headings and pictures, to locate and understand specific information (Reading strategies)

Northern Ireland Curriculum

Talking and Listening	Express thoughts, feelings and opinions in response to personal experiences, imaginary situations, literature, media and curricular topics and activities
Reading	Use a range of strategies to identify unfamiliar words
	Explore and begin to understand how texts are structured in a range of genres

An A–Z of Record Breakers

About this book
In this book, children will find an alphabetically organized selection of amazing and diverse record-breaking feats.

You will need
- *Fact cards* Photocopy Master, *Teaching Handbook* for Year 2/P3

Before reading

- Ask the children what a record breaker is. Have they ever seen books or TV programmes about record breakers? **(activating prior knowledge)**
- Look at the cover of the book. What does the title tell us about how the information in the book might be organized? What sort of information might it contain? What does the picture show? **(predicting)**

Assessment point
Can the children make predictions about a text using a range of clues?

- Look at the contents page. How does this support their ideas? **(engaging readers)**
- Ask the children how they would approach reading the rest of the book. Talk about the difference between texts that have to be read in a linear way and those that don't. What sort of text is this? **(activating and building on prior knowledge)**

Assessment point
Can the children talk about the features of certain non-fiction texts?

- Before turning to pages 4 and 5, ask the children to think of a record-breaking activity for the letter 'A'. **(predicting)**
- After reading these pages, ask them to comment on the records. Are they serious or silly, dangerous or difficult? Is breaking the record more enjoyable for the record breaker or for the audience? **(personal response, including adopting a critical stance)**
- Ask the children what to do if they encounter a difficult word, modelling with an example from the book.
- Discuss with the children what to do if they struggle to understand the meaning of a word or a sentence, e.g. rereading the word or sentence again.

> *Phonic opportunity*
> - Draw attention to all of the words with the /**igh**/ phoneme: *bright, high, kite, dive, bike, miles, by, trying*. Ask children to identify the phoneme /igh/ in the words. Support children to say each phoneme and then blend the phonemes to read the word. Ask children to think of other words with the /igh/ sound.
> - You may also wish to point out some of the common exception words or practise decoding some of the challenge and context words in this book.

During reading

- Ask the children to read from page 16 to the end of the book, selecting what interests them. If they finish, they can go back to read earlier pages.
- As they read, ask them to look for a range of record-breaking attempts: one completed in another country, one completed as a team effort, one they find frightening, one they would like to do.
- Ask the children to look out for words ending in *-est* and keep a note of them as they read.

> **Assessment point**
> Can the children identify when reading does not make sense and self-corrects in order for the text to make sense?

After reading

Returning to the text

- Ask the children which records were to do with speed. **(recall, deducing, inferring, drawing conclusions)**
- Which records would they consider unpleasant or frightening? Why? **(empathizing, visualizing and other sensory interpretations)**
- Which record-breaking attempt showed or involved the most courage/the most skill/ the most training? **(deducing, inferring, drawing conclusions)**
- On page 19, what is this tiddlywink record actually for? How could another tiddlywink record be made? (e.g. the quickest time for flicking a tiddlywink over a certain distance) **(synthesizing)**

> **Assessment point**
> Can the children provide simple explanations about events or information?

Developing comprehension

- In pairs, ask one child to choose a record and decide on three questions they would like to ask the record breaker. The 'record breaker' should think about the answers in the light of the information given on the 'card'. **(questioning, determining importance)**

Assessment point
Can the children locate specific information on a given page in response to a direct question?

- Ask the children to identify the features used consistently through the book for each record: embellished alphabet letter and type of record-breaking event; 'who', 'when', 'where' categories; details; supporting picture. Discuss how effective these features are. Is there anything the children would add or change?

Assessment point
Can the children talk about the features of certain non-fiction texts?

- Give out the *Fact cards* Photocopy Master, and ask the children to fill one 'card' in with information about something they have achieved in their own life. (It does not need to be a record-breaking event!) Remind them to use the past tense to relate the event.

Assessment point
Can the children relate stories/texts to their own experiences, including story settings and incidents?

> **Developing grammar, punctuation and spelling**

- Look at the words that the children have collected with the suffix -*est*. Discuss how these are the superlative forms of adjectives. These are used when there are more than two things being compared.
- Look closely at how they are formed by adding -*est* to the end of a root word.
- Write the words *change* and *judge* on the board and ask the children for the sound that they can hear in each. Discuss how the /dj/ sound is sometimes spelt 'ge' or 'dge' at the end of words. Can they think of any other examples? (*large*, *charge*, *fudge*, *badge*)

Follow-up

Writing activities

- Support the children in carrying out interviews in (or beyond) the classroom. Using the 'card' format as on the *Fact cards* Photocopy Master, ask them to write some 'cards' to contribute to a class book of notable achievements. **(shorter writing task)**
- Following discussion, ask the children to write about something they would really like to achieve in their lives. **(longer writing task)**
- Ask the children to imagine they are Sophie Smith, the record-breaking worm charmer, and write an explanation of how they went about achieving this record. **(short writing task)**

Other literacy activities

- Look up Ashrita Furman on the Internet to see some of the records that he has broken. Could he have a whole *A–Z of Record Breakers* book to himself? Which letters would not be covered?

Cross-curricular activities

- Hold a mental maths challenge in which children go head to head with other children, or try to break their own record. **(Maths)**
- Challenge the children to see how many games of hopscotch (or other playground games) they can play during one break time. **(PE)**
- Use your current topic to generate a record-breaking activity. **(Science, DT)**
- Investigate geographical record breakers to do with the weather, natural occurrences and physical landscape features, e.g. What is the highest tree in the world? **(Geography)**